Funding Provided by
Supervisor Mark DeSaulnier
District IV
Contra Costa County
Board of Supervisors

MADAM C.J. WALKER

ENTREPRENEUR AND MILLIONAIRE

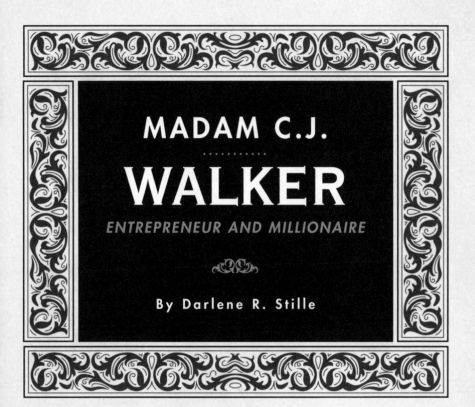

MADAM C.J.
WALKER
ENTREPRENEUR AND MILLIONAIRE

By Darlene R. Stille

Content Adviser: A'Lelia Bundles,
Great-great-granddaughter of Madam C.J. Walker,
Washington, D.C.

Reading Adviser: Rosemary G. Palmer, Ph.D.,
Department of Literacy, College of Education,
Boise State University

Compass Point Books ✦ Minneapolis, Minnesota

Compass Point Books
3109 West 50th Street, #115
Minneapolis, MN 55410

Visit Compass Point Books on the Internet at *www.compasspointbooks.com*
or e-mail your request to *custserv@compasspointbooks.com*

Editors: Sue Vander Hook, Mari Bolte
Page Production: Blue Tricycle
Photo Researcher: Svetlana Zhurkin
Cartographer: XNR Productions, Inc.
Library Consultant: Kathleen Baxter

Art Director: Jaime Martens
Creative Director: Keith Griffin
Editorial Director: Carol Jones
Managing Editor: Catherine Neitge

Library of Congress Cataloging-in-Publication Data
Stille, Darlene R.
  Madam C.J. Walker : entrepreneur and millionaire / by Darlene R. Stille.
    p. cm. — (Signature lives)
  Includes bibliographical references and index.
  ISBN-13: 978-0-7565-1883-7 (library binding)
  ISBN-10: 0-7565-1883-0 (library binding)
  ISBN-13: 978-0-7565-2203-2 (paperback)
  ISBN-10: 0-7565-2203-X (paperback)
1. Walker, C. J., Madam, 1867-1919—Juvenile literature. 2. Cosmetics
industry—United States—History—Juvenile literature. 3. African
American women executives—Biography—Juvenile literature.
4. Executives—United States—Biography—Juvenile literature. I. Title.
II. Series.
  HD9970.5.C672W3577 2007
  338.7'66855092—dc22 [B]   2006027074

MODERN AMERICA

Starting in the late 19th century, advancements in all areas of human activity transformed an old world into a new and modern place. Inventions prompted rapid shifts in lifestyle, and scientific discoveries began to alter the way humanity viewed itself. Beginning with World War I, warfare took place on a global scale, and ideas such as nationalism and communism showed that countries were taking a larger view of their place in the world. The combination of all these changes continues to produce what we know as the modern world.

Table of Contents

SELF-MADE WOMAN 9

BLEAK BEGINNINGS 15

VICKSBURG WASHERWOMAN 23

NEW START IN ST. LOUIS 29

A NEW FRONTIER 37

GROWING A BUSINESS 45

THE WALKER
MANUFACTURING COMPANY 53

WOMAN OF INFLUENCE 75

THE NEW YORK YEARS 85

LIFE AND TIMES 96
LIFE AT A GLANCE 102
ADDITIONAL RESOURCES 103
GLOSSARY 105
SOURCE NOTES 106
SELECT BIBLIOGRAPHY 108
INDEX 109
IMAGE CREDITS 112

1 SELF-MADE WOMAN

⤜⧉⤛

"Perseverance is my motto," said the self-confident and beautifully dressed African-American woman. A crowd of about 200 women listened intently as she continued:

> It [perseverance] gave us the telegraph, telephone, and wireless. It gave to the world an Abraham Lincoln, and to a race freedom.

The speaker was American entrepreneur and businesswoman Madam C.J. Walker, who had created her own line of hair-care products for black women. Her audience on that August day in 1917 was a group of women who sold Walker products and practiced what was called the Walker Method of beauty culture.

Madam C.J. Walker was a self-made millionaire who earned her fortune selling hair-care products for African-Americans.

Madam C.J. Walker was not the only African-American woman to manufacture hair products in the early 1900s. Annie Pope-Turnbo founded the Poro Company, headquartered in St. Louis, Missouri, and Chicago, Illinois. Madame Sarah Spencer Washington founded the Apex Hair and News Company in Atlantic City, New Jersey.

The Walker System was a technique that used special products and hot combs to smooth and straighten hair. There was also shampoo, hair oil, perfume, toothpaste, soap, powder, and rouge—all designed especially for black women.

Walker was speaking at the first convention of the Madam C.J. Walker Hair Culturists Union of America held at the Union Baptist Church in Philadelphia, Pennsylvania. The Walker sales agents paid rapt attention as this self-made woman shared her ideas about how to become successful in life. By then, Madam C.J. Walker was one of the wealthiest women in the United States. She encouraged the women in her audience with these words:

There is no royal flower-strewn road to success, and if there is, I have not found it, for what success I have obtained is the result of many sleepless nights and real hard work.

Walker had known what hard work was from the time she was a young girl on a plantation in Louisiana.

Her first job was picking cotton with her parents in a hot, dusty field. She learned to do laundry for white families and later became a full-time washerwoman.

As Walker sweated over washtubs, her scalp itched fiercely. Day by day, her scalp problems worsened, and then her hair began to fall out. Her situation seemed hopeless, but she searched for a cure. She came up with an idea and a product that not only healed her scalp but also freed her from a life of slavelike work. One day, her business would make her a wealthy woman.

Madam C.J. Walker (front center, in tiered dress) posed with her sales agents at the first convention of the Madam C.J. Walker Hair Culturists Union of America. To the left of Walker is her attorney F.B. Ransom; to the right is Alice Kelly, forelady of the company.

Walker developed a method for treating itchy, infected scalps and for growing back hair that had fallen out. Her method grew into an entire line of beauty products for African-American women. She worked hard to expand her business and taught other black women how to treat hair and go into business for themselves by selling her products. Working as Walker agents enabled thousands of African-American women to earn far more than they had made as washerwomen or household servants.

Madam C.J. Walker never stopped working hard. Her efforts eventually made her the first African-American female millionaire. As a nationally known business leader, she would influence and be influenced by black artists, educators, poets, and politicians. She would generously contribute part of her wealth to help African-Americans gain racial equality and to support other causes that she deemed worthy. By personal example, Walker brought hope and optimism to many black women and furthered the cause of civil rights.

2 BLEAK BEGINNINGS

Chapter

ᘓᕟᔕᕟᘛ

Madam C.J. Walker was born Sarah Breedlove on December 23, 1867. Her birthplace was a one-room shack in Delta, Louisiana, on a small cotton plantation called Grand View. Her parents, Owen and Minerva Breedlove, had been slaves there. When the Civil War ended in 1865, they stayed at the plantation, as many other freed African-Americans did at that time. Where they once picked cotton as slaves, they now picked cotton as sharecroppers.

Life was not easy for former slaves who remained in the South. Although they were free, many of them had nowhere to go. Because it had been against the law in the South for slaves to receive an education, most couldn't read or write. Some, like the Breedloves,

After the Civil War ended in 1865, thousands of former slaves stayed on farms and plantations to work as sharecroppers.

became sharecroppers, which meant they didn't own the land they farmed. They bought seeds and farming supplies from the landowner, and took a share of the profits when the crops were sold.

Robert W. Burney, the owner of Grand View, once held the Breedloves as slaves. But now he paid them to grow cotton on part of his plantation. Some years, the fields produced abundant cotton crops. Other years, crops failed from disease or insects.

In 1869, two years after Sarah was born, the cotton crop was abundant. Sarah's parents earned enough to care for their growing family as well as pay the $100 fee for their marriage. Slaves had not been allowed to legally marry. By 1869, when they were wed as free people, Owen and Minerva already had six children. The oldest was 15 years old, and the youngest was 2 months.

In Sarah Breedlove's world, there was little time for play. Sarah helped make meals, picked vegetables from the garden, and fed the chickens. She and her siblings spent the rest of the day picking cotton in the fields with their parents. The Breedloves also took in dirty laundry from white families. On Saturdays,

Cotton was one of the most important crops in Louisiana before and immediately after the Civil War. In 1860, almost one-third of the cotton exported from the United States to factories in Great Britain and France came from plantations in Louisiana.

Sarah and her sister Louvenia helped their mother wash clothes outdoors in big wooden tubs. Together, they earned about a dollar a week.

Sarah and her family faced other problems besides poverty. In the years after the war, the South was rebuilding and healing from the scars of hard-fought battles. Many white Southerners didn't like African-Americans being free, and racial tension grew.

The town of Delta had been damaged terribly

Before washing machines were invented, women washed clothes by hand. They boiled them and then scrubbed them on the ridged surface of a washboard.

during the war. Grand View plantation was across the Mississippi River from the city of Vicksburg, Mississippi. From the riverbank, the Breedloves had a wonderful view of Vicksburg. They could see smoke-belching steamboats coming and going from the busy docks, and they watched churning paddlewheels propel big boats up and down the river.

Because it was an important river port, Vicksburg had been a prime target of Union forces during the Civil War. Owen and Minerva had probably watched as Union troops set up cannons on the plantation. They would have heard the deafening booms of mortars and cannons and seen the terrible flash of exploding shells as troops fired on Vicksburg. Union troops tried to

Ulysses S. Grant attempted to capture Vicksburg from October 1962 to July 1863.

divert the waters of the Mississippi away from the docks at Vicksburg by digging a canal through Grand View. A big, muddy ditch marked their unsuccessful effort.

Like many other slaves and owners, the Breedloves and the Burneys fled from the battle in July 1863. When the fighting ended, Vicksburg was in ruins. The Breedloves had returned to Grand View, which had become a refugee camp for people whose homes had been destroyed in the fighting. Thousands of homeless African-Americans were now living in horribly crowded conditions at Grand View until they could resettle somewhere else.

Despite the hardships of war, the Breedloves hoped life would improve. After the war, the federal government made some changes to help former slaves. In 1870, African-American men were granted the right to vote, but they were often barred from doing so by hostile whites. It was also no longer illegal to educate black people in the South.

The Confederacy depended on steamboats and ferries crossing the Mississippi River to link its three western states—Arkansas, Louisiana, and Texas—with its eastern states. Union General Ulysses S. Grant wanted to capture Vicksburg, Mississippi, and take control of river traffic. Union troops had been unsuccessful, so Grant decided to starve the Confederates out. On May 18, 1863, he laid siege to Vicksburg. No one could go in or out of the city. Then Union forces fired cannons at the city. Vicksburg residents moved into caves for protection. The siege ended on July 4, 1863 when the Confederates were forced to surrender.

The Breedloves believed that through education, Sarah and their other children could have a better life. Sarah looked forward to going off to school. She was an intelligent child who was eager to learn.

Sarah, however, discovered that getting an education was nearly impossible for black children in the South. Many white Southerners wouldn't accept African-Americans as equals and tried to stop black children from attending school. Some whites formed groups to terrorize and intimidate blacks. They burned down schools that black children attended and sometimes killed teachers and students.

Sarah also learned that there wasn't much time for a sharecropper's child to go to school. Working in the cotton fields and over laundry tubs filled most of her days. By 1875, Sarah's dream of going to school slipped even further away when a double tragedy struck the Breedlove family. Tuberculosis, yellow fever, cholera, and other infectious diseases were constant threats in the hot, humid Louisiana area along the Mississippi River. Swarms of mosquitoes and polluted water carried unseen germs. Both her mother and father fell victims to a disease, perhaps cholera, and died. The Breedlove children were left alone to make a living as best they could.

Despite their hard work, the children didn't make enough money to keep up with the expenses of living in their small cabin. Three older brothers—Alex,

Sarah Breedlove lived in a cabin on the Burney plantation in Delta, Louisiana, until her parents died when she was 8 years old.

Owen Jr., and James—left to find work in Vicksburg. Three years later, in 1878, more bad luck struck the Breedlove children. The cotton crop failed. Now they had no income, and there was no other work they could do to earn money.

In addition, violence against blacks was increasing. That year, more than 70 African-Americans near Delta were murdered, mostly by hanging. Sarah and her siblings packed up their few belongings and crossed the Mississippi River to Vicksburg. They hoped life would be better there. ᥩ

3 VICKSBURG WASHERWOMAN

❦

At first, Sarah's life in Vicksburg was no better than it had been in Delta. Louvenia married a man named Jesse Powell, and Sarah lived with them. Jesse didn't like that arrangement, and Sarah complained that Jesse was mean and cruel. She longed for the day when she could afford to live somewhere else.

Sarah earned money by washing clothes for white families. Few jobs, other than picking cotton, were worse than doing laundry in the late 1800s. There were no washing machines or dryers. Clothes, towels, sheets, and tablecloths were put into tubs filled with boiling water and harsh lye soap. To get out dirt and stains, Sarah scrubbed the laundry on a washboard, a wooden frame that held a sheet of tin with ridges. The rubbing scraped her knuckles raw if

When a washerwoman finished washing laundry by hand, she hung it on a clothesline to dry.

Following the Civil
War was a period
called Reconstruction.
The goal was to bring
Southern states back
into the Union.
Federal troops went to
Southern states to
protect the rights
of black people. Many
Southerners resented
the federal government
interfering in state
affairs. Reconstruction
ended in 1877, after
all Confederate states
were readmitted to
the Union. Southern
states then passed laws
that greatly limited
the rights of African-
Americans.

she wasn't careful.

After boiling the clothes, Sarah lifted the hot, wet wash out with wooden paddles and hung it on clotheslines to dry. Then she used heavy irons heated on a stove to smooth out wrinkles in sheets, shirts, pants, and skirts. When she was finished, she folded the laundry and put it into big baskets. Sometimes she carried the baskets on her head to return the clean laundry. Other times, she pushed them in a cart.

It seemed impossible for Sarah to get ahead in Vicksburg. Still hanging over her like a dark cloud was prejudice against black people.

From the end of the Civil War through part of the 1870s, federal troops had been stationed in Southern states to protect African-Americans. But after the soldiers left, there was no one to protect them. Some African-Americans were shot, hanged, and beaten, and no one did anything about it. Many people started to look for other places to live. Kansas seemed to be the answer.

Sarah's brother Alex listened to claims about the good life in Kansas. He heard that land was cheap, black men could vote, and racists wouldn't threaten him or other African-Americans.

Members of the Ku Klux Klan wore masks and robes to hide their identities when they abused or murdered black people.

Hundreds of black families hoping for a new life boarded Mississippi River steamboats bound for St. Louis, Missouri. From there, they would head west across Missouri to Kansas. Alex joined them, and soon brothers Owen Jr. and James followed. But instead of going on to Kansas as they had originally planned, Sarah's brothers settled in St. Louis.

No one knows why, but Sarah stayed in Vicksburg with Louvenia and Jesse. Sarah's only hope of escape from this difficult situation was to get married. "I married at the age of fourteen," she later said in a matter-of-fact way, "in order to get a home of my own." The man she married was Moses McWilliams, and she was now Sarah McWilliams. Moses worked as a laborer at whatever jobs he could find. Sarah never spoke about love for her husband. She probably married him to get away from her sister's cruel husband.

African-Americans fled the South and immigrated to Kansas and other Northern states in the late 1800s.

Sarah's greatest joy came in 1885 when she was 17 years old. She and Moses had a baby girl. They named her Lelia. Sarah's daughter became the center of her life. She dreamed of having enough money to send Lelia to school and give her all the things she had never had.

Life for the next two years was good for the McWilliams family. The cotton harvests were abundant, and most of the people in Vicksburg had money for clothes, shoes, and sometimes luxuries. But just as life was getting better for Sarah, her husband died. Historians don't know for sure what happened to Moses. There were rumors that he was murdered. Some thought he died in an accident.

> *Benjamin "Pap" Singleton was a leader of the movement to settle African-Americans in Kansas in the late 1800s. It was called the Black Exodus. Thousands of African-Americans settled in colonies that Singleton established and in other all-black towns in the state. About 25,000 former slaves eventually left the South and settled in Kansas. The Black Exodus leaders believed that owning land and farming, not education, were the keys to African-American success.*

With Moses gone, Sarah didn't know what to do. She had a daughter to support. How could she make enough money? One thing was sure: She would not go back to live with Louvenia and Jesse.

4 NEW START IN ST. LOUIS

ornamental divider

Sarah McWilliams knew what she had to do—leave Vicksburg. "I was left a widow at the age of twenty with a little girl to raise," she recalled. She purchased tickets for herself and 4-year-old Lelia to go to St. Louis, where Sarah's brothers lived.

When Sarah and Lelia arrived in 1889, they found St. Louis very different from Vicksburg. While Vicksburg depended on cotton crops, St. Louis was a center of industry. Trolley cars clanged along streets made of brick. Many downtown buildings were constructed of stone, not wood. Even the air was different. It smelled bad because of the soot and smoke from the city's foundries and factories.

Fortunately, Sarah's brothers were there to help her and Lelia. They had opened their own barbershop,

When Sarah McWilliams went to St. Louis in 1889, the streets bustled with people, trolley cars, and horse-drawn carriages.

and business was good. Working as barbers was one way African-American men could get ahead in the years after the Civil War. Their barbershop was about a block away from the St. Paul African Methodist Episcopal (AME) Church, which would become an important influence on Sarah's life.

Sarah McWilliams was deeply religious, and she believed in the power of prayer. She often prayed for deliverance from her life of drudgery as a laundress. There were better-paying jobs in factories and as servants in the homes of wealthy white people. But these jobs usually went to white immigrants when they arrived from Europe.

Housing was also a problem. The only place McWilliams could afford to rent was in a neighborhood filled with saloons, pool halls, and loud dance halls. Sounds of toe-tapping ragtime and jazz tunes drifted from these places at all hours of the day and night. Unemployed men hung out on the streets, and fights often broke out as they took out their anger on each other. Sometimes, when money was scarce and she couldn't afford to pay her rent, McWilliams moved in with one of her brothers.

One refuge in her life was the AME church. Founded in the early 1800s, the AME group of churches had been involved for many years in social and political issues. During the Civil War, church members in the North had worked to abolish slavery.

After the war, AME churches worked to better the lives of its African-American members.

Many middle-class black women in the St. Louis church helped McWilliams. Not all African-Americans were poor like she was. In fact, some were quite prosperous. Free blacks in the North had learned to read and write, and many had attended college. Some were teachers, doctors, and lawyers. Others owned their own businesses. But even though they were successful, they still weren't accepted in white society. They formed their own organizations, such as social clubs and churches. Although McWilliams couldn't join middle-class social clubs, she felt welcome in the church.

Groups of unemployed men hung out on the streets of St. Louis with little to do.

> Social clubs were an important part of middle-class life in the early 1900s. Women's clubs held social gatherings, helped establish libraries, and worked on other community projects. Most clubs accepted only white people. African-Americans started their own clubs, such as the Black Freemasons and the Colored Knights of Pythias, which had a women's auxiliary called the Court of Calanthe.

At church, McWilliams met well-dressed, wealthy African-American men and women. The women wore fine, long dresses and big hats adorned with artificial flowers and feathers. McWilliams was always neatly dressed, but her clothes were patched and shabby. It must have given her hope to see prosperous African-Americans.

One middle-class church member was Sarah Cohron, a graduate of Oberlin College and founder of the St. Louis Colored Orphans Home. She considered McWilliams' daughter, Lelia, to be a half-orphan because her father was dead. She invited Lelia to live at the orphanage part of the week.

This form of child care must have been a great help to McWilliams while she carried her bundles of wash to and from the homes of her customers. She was pleased that Lelia could go to school with other children. She began saving money from her small earnings with the hope that Lelia could someday attend college. McWilliams also wanted to go to school. Later, she would enroll in night classes in St. Louis and learn the basics of reading and writing.

As poor as she was, McWilliams still believed in giving to others. She joined St. Paul's missionary society, a group dedicated to helping the needy. One of the first things she did was collect money for a poor black man, his blind sister, and sick wife.

Outside church, McWilliams' life sometimes was filled with sadness. Her brother Alex died in 1893, leaving a widow and four children. Her sister Louvenia's son, Willie, was convicted of manslaughter and sent to prison. In 1894, McWilliams married a man named John Davis, who drank heavily and refused to work. After nine years of marriage, they separated, and Sarah went back to using the name Sarah McWilliams.

There seemed to be no way for McWilliams to succeed and provide for her daughter. She later remembered:

I was at my washtubs one morning with a heavy wash before me ... As I bent over the washboard, and looked at my arms buried in soapsuds, I said to myself: "What are you going to do when you grow old and your back gets stiff? Who is going to take care of your little girl?" This set me to thinking, but with all my thinking I couldn't see how I, a poor washerwoman, was going to better my condition.

Adding to her woes was the fact that her scalp itched constantly. McWilliams scratched her head until it bled. Then her hair began to fall out. Bald patches revealed a bare head covered with red, bleeding sores. How embarrassed she must have been joining 900 members of her church on a Sunday morning with a cloth tied around her head to hide her condition.

Sarah McWilliams wasn't alone in her suffering. Many women had severe scalp conditions. The popular belief at the time was that shampooing was not good for the hair. Left unwashed, the scalp developed severe dandruff caused by flakes of dead skin. McWilliams' problem was growing worse.

McWilliams tried many kinds of hair remedies, but none of them helped. In 1902, a woman named Annie Pope-Turnbo arrived in St. Louis with a new hair-care product that she claimed would grow hair. Pope-Turnbo went door-to-door selling her hair grower as part of the Poro line of hair-care products. The first step to a healthy scalp, she taught, was to wash the hair and get rid of dandruff.

The year after McWilliams met Pope-Turnbo, she became a Poro agent and began to sell the product door-to-door. McWilliams was a hard worker, and she realized her hard work might pay off. She could make far more money as a Poro saleswoman than as a laundress, and she seized the opportunity. She said:

When I was a washerwoman, I was considered a good washerwoman and laundress ... but, work as I would, I seldom could make more than $1.50 a day. I got my start by giving myself a start.

Selling Poro products would introduce McWilliams to the world of hair care.

By 1905, McWilliams felt she needed to start over in a new city. She chose Denver, Colorado, as her future home. ❧

5 A NEW FRONTIER

⚬୧⌇ଵ⚬

Sarah McWilliams arrived in Denver on July 20, 1905. She may have chosen Denver because her sister-in-law and four nieces were there. Twenty-year-old Lelia didn't come with her mother because she was now attending Knoxville College in Tennessee. McWilliams didn't have much money for her new beginning in Colorado. After she bought her train ticket, she had only $1.50 left over.

Denver was very different from St. Louis. McWilliams breathed in crisp, clean air instead of soot and pollution. The snow-capped Rocky Mountains rose on the horizon to the west. Denver was still a frontier town whose residents had come seeking fortunes in gold, silver, and land. About 10,000 black people lived in Denver, where slavery

As Sarah McWilliams became more successful, she sported finer clothes, including a seal fur coat.

A panoramic view of down-town Denver, Colorado, in 1906 showed the Rocky Mountains in the background.

had never been legal. It was a much better place for blacks than St. Louis, where people were more prejudiced. Denver seemed like a good place for an African-American woman to start a new business.

McWilliams began selling Poro products and worked as a cook at a boardinghouse. She saved as much money as possible so she could start her own business—her own line of hair-care products. No one knows for sure, but McWilliams may have received help from Edmund L. Scholtz, who owned the largest drugstore in Denver. He may have stayed for a short time at the boardinghouse where McWilliams worked. Many have wondered if she asked his advice about chemical ingredients for her hair grower. Some speculate he may have analyzed the ingredients in the Poro products and suggested how she could make them better.

Sarah McWilliams, however, said she developed her hair grower with divine help. She claimed it happened in a dream:

> *A big black man appeared to me and told me what to mix up for my hair. Some of the remedy was grown in Africa, but I sent for it, mixed it up, put it on my scalp, and in a few weeks my hair was coming in faster than it had ever fallen out. I made up my mind I would begin to sell it.*

Sulfur was one of the secret ingredients in Madam C.J. Walker's Wonderful Hair Grower. Since ancient times, sulfur, a chemical element, has been used in medicines. It can kill the germs that cause infections of the skin and is still used in some shampoos.

She kept her formula a closely guarded secret.

By November, McWilliams had saved enough money to quit her job as a cook. To make ends meet, she washed laundry two days a week. But her main focus was her hair products. She rented a space and opened a laboratory where customers could see how her product could grow hair. Then she began to network, or connect, with people who might help her business grow. She joined an AME church and built relationships with people who would soon become part of her business. She joined women's groups and social clubs that would help promote her hair products to potential buyers.

It was easier to join social clubs in Denver than in St. Louis. Clubs in St. Louis welcomed mainly well-to-do, educated, middle-class people. In Denver, however, everyone was welcome. They were all newcomers in similar circumstances—striving for a decent life and sometimes wealth.

McWilliams put most of the money she earned back into her business by advertising in black newspapers. An ad in 1905 read, "Mrs. McWilliams, formerly of St. Louis, has special rates for a month to demonstrate her ability to grow hair."

That month, a man McWilliams had befriended in St. Louis joined her in Denver. His name was Charles Joseph Walker, but his friends called him C.J. A sociable man about town, Walker was full of ideas and was a perfect partner for McWilliams' new business. He would also become her partner in marriage. McWilliams became his wife on January 4, 1906. She now called herself Madam C.J. Walker.

Madam Walker continued to work tirelessly in her new business venture. She mixed and tested

When Sarah McWilliams married C.J. Walker, she chose to use the title "Madam" for several reasons. Madam was similar to the French word madame, which Americans associated with elegance and high fashion. Also, it lent an aura of dignity and authority to this African-American businesswoman.

products in her spare time, giving them names such as Wonderful Hair Grower, Brilliantine, and Glossine. Each container showed a picture of Walker and her long, thick hair. When she went out to sell, she carried products in a businesslike black case and dressed professionally in a starched blouse and long skirt.

Walker often gave free demonstrations to get people to buy her products. Sometimes there were several women at a presentation, and other times there was only one. She began by washing a woman's hair with Vegetable Shampoo. Keeping the hair and scalp clean was very important to prevent hair loss. Then she applied her Wonderful Hair Grower to

One of Walker's most popular products was her Wonderful Hair Grower. The picture of Walker on the container showed how the product would make hair straight and smooth.

lessen dandruff and heal sores. The final step in the treatment involved a heated steel comb. Walker first rubbed oil into the hair and then used a hot comb to relax and soften the tight curls. She called her system the Madam Walker Hair Culture Method.

The more Walker demonstrated her products, the more confidence she gained. She found that she had a talent for entertaining audiences as well as convincing them to buy her goods. Women began flocking to Madam Walker, drawn by her products and outgoing personality.

C.J. Walker knew how to promote and advertise his wife's products. In the early 1900s, some ads made wild claims, and no one checked to see if they were valid. To show that the ads for Wonderful Hair Grower were true, he printed before and after pictures of Madam Walker's hair.

Two newspapers carried Walker's ads for her mail-order business, inviting people to mail in their orders for hair-care products. As orders poured in, the Walkers mailed out products to their eager customers. Within a few months, sales reached $10 a week, a very respectable sum for those days.

Madam Walker was just beginning to see how successful her business could be. She traveled to other towns in Colorado and then to other states to sell her products. Her husband and friends feared she would spend more than she earned. Madam Walker,

BEFORE USING

however, proved them wrong. Sales began to soar.

In 1906, Lelia graduated from Knoxville College and joined her mother in Denver. At the age of 21, standing 6 feet (183 centimeters) tall in heels, Lelia was poised and elegant. She began working for her mother, helping her cousins fill orders for hair-care products.

That year, Madam Walker set out on a sales trip to nine states. Lelia and her cousins stayed in Denver, barely able to keep up with orders that arrived by mail. Sales grew, and Walker was now earning twice as much as the average white male. And she was just getting started. ✤

The earliest known photograph of Walker displayed the effects of her Wonderful Hair Grower in before and after shots.

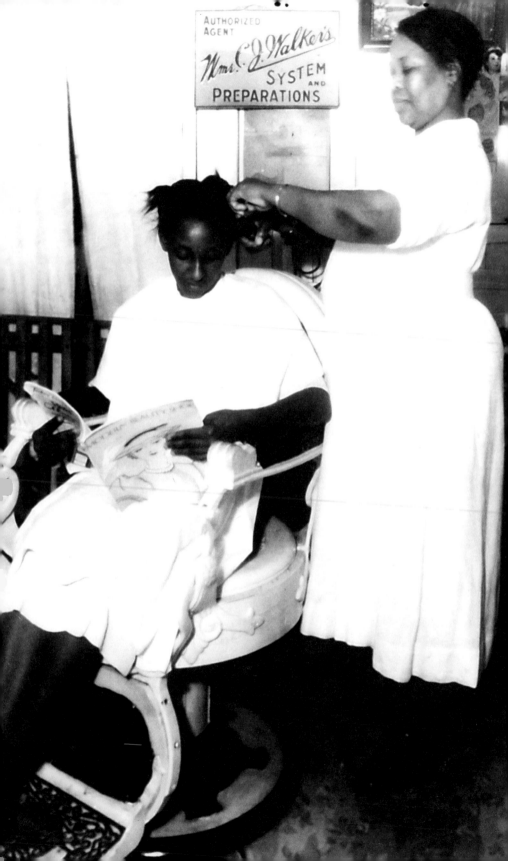

6 GROWING A BUSINESS

❦❧

When C.J. Walker saw how many orders were coming in from his wife's successful nine-state trip, he decided to make his own products. He developed Walker's Sore Wash and Walker's Sure Cure Blood and Rheumatic Cure. Unlike Madam Walker's products, however, there was no evidence that his remedies and tonics worked, and his business didn't succeed.

Madam Walker had shown her products could grow hair, and she set out to grow her company even more. She and C.J. began traveling around the country, recruiting agents to sell Wonderful Hair Grower and other merchandise. When they arrived in a town, they visited local churches, especially Baptist and AME churches. They also contacted African-American social clubs and organizations.

Beauty salons became more popular all over the country. Some people set up salons in their homes.

Madam Walker held free demonstrations for these groups and took orders for her hair-care supplies. Above all, she recruited new agents to sell Walker products in their communities. She trained her agents in the Walker Hair Culture, a method of cleaning and treating scalps and using a heated steel comb.

Many of the women at the demonstrations had grown up on Southern farms. Walker spoke to them in terms they understood. "Do you realize that it is as necessary to cultivate the scalp to grow hair as it is to cultivate the soil to grow a garden?" she often began. "If the grass is removed and the soil cultivated, the plant will be a very healthy one. The same applies

Madam Walker (seated third from right) with her Ohio sales agents

to the scalp." Walker assured them that "every woman who wants hair can have it, no matter how short, how stubby, or what the condition of the scalp may be."

Walker's treatments caught on like wildfire. African-American women needed help with their hair, and her products helped. Walker received letters from customers who praised her discovery. They shared personal stories of how her products helped their hair. A Dallas, Texas, woman wrote:

> All the people who know me are just wild about my hair. ... I have to take it down to let them see and feel it ... I tell you I am quite an advertisement here for your goods.

> In the late 1800s and early 1900s there was a rapidly growing business in what was called patent medicines. Ads for these medicines made outrageous claims. It seemed there was nothing they could not cure, from baldness to cancer. The truth was that these concoctions contained dangerous substances, such as lead, cocaine, mercury, and opium. Concern about the dangers and abuses of these medicines was part of the reason Congress passed the Food and Drug Act in 1906.

Not only did Walker find a way to satisfy women's hair-care needs, she also found a way to help them economically. In 1906, black women who worked as servants for wealthy white families made $8 to $20 a month. The less fortunate made about $6 a month doing laundry. Madam Walker knew firsthand how difficult this work was. She promised her agents they could make more by selling her products. They would also gain dignity by not having to work as servants. She later stated, "I have made it possible for many colored women to abandon the wash-tub for more pleasant and profitable occupation."

Orders flowing into Denver were more than Walker's operation could handle. She decided to move the business to a more central location where it would be easier to ship out goods. When Walker and her husband visited Pittsburgh, Pennsylvania, in the summer of 1907, they saw a grimy, industrial city, but they knew it would be ideal for their growing mail-order business. Sixteen railroad lines came together

The Duquesne steel factory in Pittsburgh, Pennsylvania, was one of the city's many industries in the early 1900s.

there to deliver coal and ore to foundries and to transport iron and steel. Pittsburgh was an ideal place from which to send packages to every state.

In 1908, the Walkers moved to Pittsburgh, and Madam Walker started networking with black churches and social clubs. She persuaded community leaders to sign a petition endorsing her products. She also opened a beauty salon. By 1909, she was earning the equivalent of $150,000 a year in today's dollars.

Then Madam Walker and her daughter came up with an idea that would move the business another step forward. They opened a school in Pittsburgh to train Walker agents. Walker named it Lelia College in honor of her daughter. In 1908, Lelia moved from Denver to Pittsburgh to help run the school. Women who successfully completed the Lelia College course received a graduation diploma and could call themselves hair culturists. They were also allowed to sell Walker products and open beauty salons that practiced the Walker method of treating hair.

Before the Civil War, Pittsburgh was an important "depot," or destination, for the Underground Railroad. The Underground Railroad was a network of routes that escaped slaves followed to find safety in the North. There were safe houses along the way where they could stay and rest. Many escaped slaves settled in Pittsburgh. By 1910, Pittsburgh's black population ranked fifth among Northern cities.

Walker taught her agents how to pamper themselves and feel special and beautiful. But she also gave them a deeper meaning of beauty. In a Walker textbook, her agents read:

> *To be beautiful ... does not refer alone to the arrangement of the hair, the perfection of the complexion or to the beauty of the form. ... To be beautiful, one must combine these qualities with a beautiful mind and soul; a beautiful character.*

One graduate wrote:

> *You have opened up a trade for hundreds of colored women to make an honest and profitable living where they make as much in a week as a month's salary would bring from any other position that a colored woman can secure.*

Walker hair parlors began springing up all over the United States. Madam Walker was soon on the road again, recruiting agents in Ohio and nearby states. Lelia traveled to states east of Pennsylvania to locate new markets.

Lelia and her mother worked well together, but they didn't always agree. Sometimes, Lelia felt her mother was trying to run her life. In 1909, Lelia did something very much on her own—she married

N

W—E

S

C A N A D A

CANADA

Great Lakes

Wash.

Montana   N. Dak.   Minn.

N.H. Maine

Oregon

Idaho

Wyoming

South
Dakota

Wis.

Michigan

Vt.

N.Y.

Mass.

R.I.

Pa.

Conn.

Nebraska   Iowa

N.J.

Nevada

Utah

Colorado

Calif.

Kansas   Mo.

Ill.   Ind. Oh.

W.Va.

Del.

Md.

Va.

Kentucky

N.C.

Arizona
Terr.

New
Mexico
Terr.

Okla.
Terr. Ind.
Terr.

Ark.

Tenn.

S.C.

*Pacific
Ocean*

Texas

Miss.

La.

Ga.

Ala.

*Atlantic
Ocean*

Florida

Coal deposits

Iron deposits

Major railroads

● Electrical power plant

● Steel plant

Map shows boundaries
of 1900.

Gulf of Mexico

0   450 miles

MEXICO   0   450 kilometers

*Steel factories,
mining opera-
tions, and
electrical power
stations sprang
up across the
country in the
early 1900s.*

John Robinson, a man no one knew much about. Her mother didn't attend the wedding. Perhaps she didn't approve of Lelia's new husband.

Mother and daughter soon got over their differences, however, and Walker put Lelia in charge of the Pittsburgh operation. Walker believed it was time to look for an additional location for her business. This time, she was looking for land to build a factory where hair-care products could be produced in large quantities. ✍

7 The Walker Manufacturing Company

❧⦿❧

Madam Walker wanted to create a corporation that could issue stock. Her plan was to convince 100 African-American men and women to invest $50,000 in her business. Walker needed this money to build a large factory to produce her products. If the business was successful, the investors would share the profits. The factory would also provide employment for black men and women.

Walker wanted to keep the stock within the black community. She feared that certain white-owned companies would want to share in her success. They would "want me to sell out my right[s] to them," she said, "which I refuse to do."

Her supporters thought she had a wonderful plan and urged her to seek help from a man she greatly admired—Booker T. Washington. He was the founder of Tuskegee Institute, a college in Tuskegee, Alabama, that trained African-Americans to become teachers. She wrote to Washington:

> *I know I can not do any thing alone, so I have decided to make an appeal to the leaders of the race ... I feel no hesitancy in presenting my case to you, as I know you know what it is to struggle alone with the ability to do, but no money to back it.*

Washington wrote Walker a polite but rather disappointing reply:

> *My dear Madam, ... My time and attention are almost wholly occupied with the work of this institution and I do not feel that I can possibly undertake other responsibilities. I hope very much you may be successful in organizing the stock company and that you may be successful in placing upon the market your preparation.*

It was the first of several times that Washington would snub her.

Madam Walker's dream of having investors didn't come true, but she didn't let it stop her. She found enough money to go forward with her plan to build a factory.

Walker's search for a good location for her

factory and national headquarters took her to several cities, including Indianapolis, Indiana. She had to stay in private homes there, since few hotels allowed African-American guests.

Madam Walker would call many cities home throughout her career.

In Indianapolis, she and C.J. stayed at the home of Dr. Joseph Ward, who operated a hospital for African-Americans. Ward and his wife took the Walkers to many social events and to the Bethel AME Church, where they met many people.

One person they met was George L. Knox, publisher of a local newspaper, the *Indianapolis Freeman*. Knox was impressed with Walker and wanted her to settle in his city. Many of the 233,000 people living there in 1910 were African-Americans. A greater percentage of blacks lived there than in any other Northern city. The city boasted a black middle class of doctors, lawyers, teachers, and other professionals. Black-owned businesses lined Indiana Avenue.

Indianapolis was also a major industrial and transportation center. Eight major railroads carried more than a million freight cars in and out of the city every year. The city would be an ideal place for Walker's business. Knox was very persuasive, and Walker said:

> I was so impressed with [Indianapolis] and the cordial welcome extended ... that I decided to make this city my home.

That year, the Walkers moved to Indianapolis and purchased a home

Indianapolis is rich in black history. The city's Bethel African Methodist Episcopal Church served as a stop on the underground railroad, helping blacks escape slavery in the South. After the Civil War, the population of Indianapolis grew steadily. Black-owned businesses were set up to serve the growing community. By 1910, about 10 percent of the city's population was black. Although they still faced a great deal of discrimination, the quality of life in Indianapolis tended to make the city attractive to middle-class African-Americans, such as Madam C.J. Walker.

Walker's home in Indianapolis, Indiana, was also a salon.

as well as a piece of land for a factory. Orders for Walker products poured in as a result of newspaper ads and successful agents across the country. Walker worked hard and continued to put money back into her business. She needed more money to build her factory, so she opened up a beauty parlor and rented out rooms to boarders in her new home. She also did her own cooking and laundry to save money.

Walker could no longer handle the expanding business on her own. She needed people with special skills, especially those with legal expertise. She hired two young black attorneys to work for her, Robert Lee Brokenburr and Freeman B. Ransom. Brokenburr was made responsible for the legal work that set up the Madam C.J. Walker Manufacturing Company as a corporation, naming Madam Walker, her husband C.J., and her daughter Lelia the only officers. The company would eventually employ more than 3,000 African-American men and women. It would become the largest black-owned business in the United States at that time.

Freeman B. Ransom was an influential businessman and an active member in the NAACP.

Walker's factory in Indianapolis produced hair- and skin-care products that were shipped to customers who ordered items through the mail.

Ransom stayed in Madam Walker's home, giving her legal advice in exchange for room and board. Eventually, he became the corporation's general manager and one of the key people in Walker's business. Brokenburr became Walker's assistant manager. He worked part time so he could continue his law practice. Eventually, he would enter politics, and in 1941, he became an Indiana state senator.

After making sure the Indianapolis operation was running smoothly, Madam Walker began traveling again. In her presentations, she still talked about her hair-care products, but now she showed slides that highlighted the accomplishments of other African-Americans. The slide show made her talks more exciting, and she often spoke to packed houses.

Walker's business was doing well and

making a good profit, but she didn't keep all the money for herself. She was generous and gave to causes she felt were important. One cause she believed in was education for black young people. She was determined to help them get the formal education she had never had.

In 1912, Walker met well-known educator Mary McLeod Bethune at a National Association of Colored Women's conference. In 1904, Bethune had founded the Daytona Normal and Industrial Institute for Negro Girls (now Bethune-Cookman College) in Florida. Within two years of founding the school, Bethune had 250 students. Before that, there had been no school

Mary McLeod Bethune (third from left) and students prepared a meal at Daytona Normal and Industrial Institute.

for Florida's black children. Walker saw that they shared the vision of educating black women and admired Bethune's perseverance. Walker helped raise money for the school and, in 1916, started a course there in hair culture. Bethune and Walker admired each other very much and became lifelong friends.

Walker also traveled outside the United States, recruiting new agents and setting up hair salons on Caribbean islands and in Central America. In addition, she looked for talent to add to her staff at the Indianapolis headquarters.

Since Walker had never been able to get a good education, she needed well-educated people to take leadership roles in her business. Walker could read and write a little, but she knew she would need to depend on other people for those skills.

While traveling in Kentucky, Walker met a schoolteacher named Alice Kelly. Walker trained her and made her forelady, or supervisor,

Mary McLeod Bethune (1875–1955) was born to former slaves in South Carolina. Educated at religious schools, including Moody Bible Institute in Chicago, Illinois, Bethune became one of the leading African-American educators in the United States. Concerned with education and equal rights for African-American women, she founded a school for black girls in 1904 in Daytona, Florida. The school eventually became a coeducational school called Bethune-Cookman College. Bethune worked to end discrimination in education and became the first black woman to head a federal agency, the Division of Negro Affairs of the National Youth Administration.

Mary McLeod Bethune stood with a line of students at Daytona Normal and Industrial Institute for Negro Girls.

of the Indianapolis factory. Kelly was well-educated and well-mannered. Walker counted on her to write letters, prepare speeches, and give her advice on etiquette. Kelly became so important to the business that Walker entrusted her with the secret hair-growing formula.

One of Kelly's former students, Violet Davis Reynolds, became Walker's private secretary. Two bookkeepers also joined the staff. Walker depended on them for more than business matters. When she came across a word she didn't know, she asked them what it meant or had one of them look it up in the dictionary.

Walker was also a firm supporter of the black Young Men's Christian Association, or YMCA. The YMCA movement started in London in 1844, with the intent of improving the "spiritual, mental and physical condition of young men." Many local YMCAs, however, had refused to allow African-American men to use the facility. As a result, in 1853, the first YMCA for blacks was established.

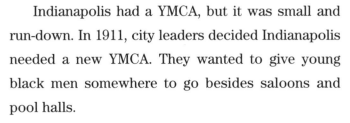

Mary McLeod Bethune became one of Madam Walker's close friends.

Indianapolis had a YMCA, but it was small and run-down. In 1911, city leaders decided Indianapolis needed a new YMCA. They wanted to give young black men somewhere to go besides saloons and pool halls.

A fund-raising campaign began in order to raise money for the new facility. Madam Walker astounded the community by being the first to pledge $1,000. That was an enormous sum in 1911 and the largest donation by any member of the African-American community—let alone by a woman. Headlines of

> The National Negro Business League was founded by Booker T. Washington with the intent to promote the "commercial, agricultural, educational, and industrial advancement" of African-Americans. The national headquarters was at Tuskegee Institute, but there were also state and local chapters. At league gatherings, prosperous African-American men and women told inspiring stories of how they had overcome obstacles to succeed in business. They suggested strategies that could help other African-American commercial groups. The National Business League has its headquarters in Washington, D.C.

black newspapers around the country praising her goodwill would help her become known as the "Best Known Hair Culturist in America."

Walker still admired Booker T. Washington, the successful black educator, although he didn't seem to return her admiration. Walker was determined, however, to win his approval for her accomplishments. She would go about this task with the same strength and determination she showed when she lifted herself up out of poverty.

Running her business, giving to worthy causes, and working for equality for African-Americans would occupy the rest of her life.

Things were going well for Walker, but her marriage to C.J. was in trouble. Often disagreeing about money and business, the two spent a great deal of time apart. They drifted further and further apart, and in 1912, they divorced. Madam Walker, then 45 years old, would never marry again.

In 1917, Walker held a convention in Philadelphia

for her own company—the first National Convention of Madam C.J. Walker Agents. She now had more than 20,000 trained agents.

She was earning record amounts of money each year. When a reporter asked about her income, she cautiously replied:

> *Well, until recently it gave me great plea-sure to tell ... the amount of money I made yearly, thinking it would inspire my hearers. But I found that for so doing some looked upon me as a boastful person who wanted to blow my own horn.*

Booker T. Washington had refused to help Madam C.J. Walker build her factory, but she still looked up to him. She agreed with his ideas that blacks needed to be educated and trained in order to get ahead. Washington and Walker both believed that blacks should live clean, virtuous lives so they could develop respect for themselves and from others.

Washington had founded the National Negro Business League in 1900 to encourage black men and women in business. At the league's annual conventions, members shared ideas and success stories with one another. Madam Walker wanted to share her story, too. Washington, however, wanted nothing to do with her.

Hair treatment was a controversial topic. Many

black women were uncomfortable with their tightly curled hair and tried to straighten it. Some white-owned cosmetic companies were selling products that straightened hair with chemicals. Washington believed these companies were taking advantage of African-American women. He said they encouraged black women to have white standards of beauty. He urged black newspapers not to carry ads for products that made black women look like white women. Perhaps he thought Madam Walker's products fell into this category.

Some leaders and their followers looked down on black women who tried to look like white women. They urged African-Americans to be proud of their heritage. Author W.E.B. DuBois called being an African-American "double-consciousness." He wrote:

> One ever feels his two-ness,
> —an American, a Negro;
> two souls, two thoughts, two
> unreconciled strivings; two
> warring ideals in one dark
> body.

Walker was determined to convince Washington that her products weren't meant to make black women look like white

Booker T. Washington (1856–1915) was born a slave in Virginia. When the Civil War ended in 1865, 9-year-old Washington had to go to work in the salt mines and coal mines to help out his very poor family. When he turned 16, he walked 200 miles (320 kilometers) to Hampton, Virginia, to attend the Hampton Institute, a school for black children. He worked as a janitor to pay his way through school and eventually became a teacher. In 1881, he founded the Tuskegee Normal and Industrial Institute, a school for blacks in Alabama. Washington believed that African-Americans should learn skills and work hard to win the respect of whites.

᪥᪥᪥

Tuskegee Institute began as a promise made by a candidate for the Alabama Senate who swore to help fund a school for blacks if they would vote for him. He kept his promise, and the Institute was founded on July 4, 1881. Booker T. Washington was hired as the school's first principal, a post he held until he died in 1915. Tuskegee became a major center for African-American education. One of its famous teachers was the scientist George Washington Carver, who discovered many uses for peanuts, such as peanut butter. The school also trained the Tuskegee Airmen, black pilots who were combat heroes of World War II. The Institute became Tuskegee University in 1985.

women. She wanted him to understand that she was helping African-American women and that her goals were the same as his. Walker knew that winning Washington's approval would benefit her and her business.

Washington planned to hold a Negro Farmers' Conference at the Tuskegee Institute in January 1912. Walker wrote a letter to Washington, asking if she could be allowed to attend, speak to the audience, and sell her products on the college grounds. She was certain Washington knew about her and her growing business. She was also certain he knew about her generous pledge to the YMCA. But instead of an invitation, Walker received a reply from Washington that ended, "Somehow I do not feel that a visit to our Conference would offer the opportunity which you seem to desire."

Walker would not take no for an answer and went to the conference anyway. She again asked Washington to let her tell her success story as an inspiration to the audience. He gave in and let her speak for 10 minutes, not at the conference but at a meeting before it began.

In August 1912, Walker was again at a conference with Washington—the annual convention of the National Negro Business League in Chicago, Illinois. Walker and her good friend George Knox, the newspaper publisher, listened to one motivational speech after another. At one point, Washington asked for comments from the audience. Knox stood up and introduced Madam C.J. Walker:

Many graduates of Tuskegee Institute became teachers. Others developed skills that qualified them for good jobs in industry and agriculture.

I arise to ask this convention for a few minutes of its time to hear a remarkable woman. ... She is the woman who gave $1,000 to the Young Men's Christian Association of Indianapolis. Madam Walker, the lady I refer to, is the manufacturer of hair goods and preparations.

Washington (seated second from left) with members of the National Negro Business League Executive Committee

Washington ignored Knox's request and called on another delegate to speak. Walker must have been furious. She knew she would have to try another strategy.

On the last day of the conference, her patience

had worn out. She stood up and boldly said to Washington, "Surely you are not going to shut the door in my face." She now had the audience's attention and added:

> *I feel that I am in a business that is a credit to the womanhood of our race. ... I went into a business that is despised, that is criticized and talked about by every-body—the business of growing hair. They did not believe such a thing could be done, but I have proven beyond the question of a doubt that I do grow hair!*

The audience laughed and applauded. Walker then made one of her most famous speeches:

> *I am a woman who came from the cotton fields of the South. I was promoted from there to the washtub. Then I was promoted to the cook kitchen, and from there I pro-moted myself into the business of manu-facturing hair goods and preparations.*

Her tone was defiant. She knew Washington didn't support her or her products. Although interrupted often by the crowd's applause, she continued:

> *I am not ashamed of my past. ... I am not ashamed of my humble beginning. Don't think because you have to go down in the wash-tub that you are any less of a lady!*

... Everybody told me I was making a mistake by going into this business, but I know how to grow hair as well as I know how to grow cotton. ... I have built my own factory on my own ground.

She told the gathering that her dream was to use her money to help others and to build a Tuskegee Institute in Africa. Washington said nothing and called on the next speaker. But Walker had, in fact, made an impression on him. He invited her to speak at the league's next annual convention.

After that, their relationship greatly improved. The Indianapolis YMCA was dedicated in 1913, and Washington was invited to be the keynote speaker. Walker invited him to stay at her home as a guest. At the dedication ceremony, Walker and Washington shared the podium. In his keynote address, Washington noted Walker's generosity and said she had a business they could all be proud of.

Washington then invited Walker to speak at the league's next annual convention. He also approved a National Negro Business League resolution declaring Walker "the foremost business woman of our race." In his speech, he praised Walker's generosity and said she had a business of which they could all be proud. In return, Walker donated scholarship money to Tuskegee Institute. The two would one day stand together at a podium for the dedication of another YMCA.

Throughout Walker's life, Washington would stay in her home as a guest. When Washington died in 1915, Walker shared how she felt about him:

Madam Walker and Washington (center) participated in the dedication of the Indianapolis YMCA in 1913.

> *I have never lost anyone, not even one of my own family that I regret more than I do the loss of this great and good man for he is not only a loss to his immediate relations and friends but to the Race and the world.* 🙘

8 WOMAN OF INFLUENCE

❧❦❧

Although Madam Walker's business kept her very busy, she found time to enjoy herself. One of her greatest pleasures was taking rides in automobiles, which were still uncommon in the early 1900s. There were far more horses and buggies, and only the wealthiest people owned cars. Walker, Lelia, and their friends often rode around in Walker's big, chauffeur-driven car. Walker would sit in the back seat with the top down in good weather. She also owned a small electric car that she drove herself.

Walker also enjoyed silent movies at the Isis Theater in downtown Indianapolis. She and her secretary, Violet Reynolds, often took off work on Saturday afternoons to sit in the darkened theater and laugh at the antics of Charlie Chaplin and gasp at

Walker sat at the wheel of her Model T Ford with her niece Anjetta Breedlove in the front seat. In the backseat are factory forelady Alice Kelly (right) and bookkeeper Lucy Flint.

daring cowboys in movies about the Old West. They sighed over romantic films as a live pianist tinkled out music to suit the mood of the pictures flashing on the silent screen.

One Saturday, Walker arrived at the Isis Theater and paid her usual dime admission. The ticket agent pushed back her 10 cents and said that admission for colored people had gone up to 25 cents. It was still a dime for white people, however. This was racial discrimination, and Walker fought back. She told her attorney, Freeman Ransom, to sue the theater for $100. There is no record of how the case turned out, but it showed how Madam Walker was willing to use her fortune and her influence to fight for racial equality.

American writer W.E.B. DuBois (1868–1963)

In the early 1900s, many African-Americans didn't agree on how to fight for equal rights. One group, led by Booker T. Washington, thought blacks shouldn't be so outspoken in their protests. Instead, the group encouraged thrift and hard work. The other group, led by author W.E.B. DuBois, believed that African-

Americans had to fight discrimination head-on. This group encouraged protests and lawsuits.

Walker was careful not to take either side. She didn't completely agree with Washington or DuBois, although they both had done great things to help black people. She wanted to support causes and not take sides with a particular leader or group.

As discrimination against blacks got worse, however, Walker began to realize that protests were an effective way to fight prejudice. Vigilantes were roaming the countryside, personally punishing blacks who, they claimed, were breaking the law. The Ku Klux Klan, a group that believes whites are superior, threatened black people and committed acts of violence against them, especially in the South.

Local laws in many Southern states made segregation legal. Blacks and whites sat in separate areas of trains, buses, and restaurants. They had separate restrooms and drinking fountains.

> *The Ku Klux Klan was founded in 1866 by veterans of the Confederate Army. Members of the group opposed equal rights for former slaves. They beat and murdered African-Americans to prevent them from voting or exercising other rights. The group nearly disappeared after President Ulysses S. Grant passed the Civil Rights Act of 1871. A second Klan that arose in 1915 opposed African-Americans as well as Roman Catholics and Jews. They held cross-burning ceremonies and committed acts of violence, such as lynchings. The Klan had about 4 million members, but it lost popularity in the late 1900s.*

Sometimes people were lynched—usually beaten and hanged—by the Ku Klux Klan and other white mobs. Almost 3,000 people were lynched between 1885 and 1917.

There were also race riots. One of the worst occurred in East St. Louis, Illinois, in 1917. Dozens of people were killed by a group of angry whites. In black neighborhoods, houses on 16 blocks were burned down.

The National Association for the Advancement of Colored People (NAACP), a civil rights organization formed in 1909, organized a march to protest the riots and all forms of mob violence. Walker joined the committee that planned the march. On July 28, 1917, thousands of African-Americans marched silently down Fifth Avenue in New York City. They carried signs that condemned the East St. Louis riot. They protested leaders who hadn't spoken out in opposition to the violence and lynchings. Even U.S. President Woodrow Wilson had refused to comment on these events.

Walker was also upset because African-American soldiers in World War I (1914–1918) weren't being treated equally. Walker, DuBois, and other leaders had helped recruit black troops for the war, and now they weren't being treated with the same respect as other soldiers.

Four days after the silent march, Walker and

other black leaders traveled to Washington, D.C., by train to meet with the president of the United States. President Wilson had agreed to meet with them, but when they arrived at the White House, they were told that the president had another appointment. The group left a petition for Wilson. It stated that 36 out

In 1917, African-American men, women, and children marched in New York City to demonstrate against the riots in East St. Louis, Illinois.

79

Woodrow Wilson was president of the United States from 1913 to 1921.

of every 100 eligible black men had joined the Army. Now the president needed to protect them and "use his great powers" to help prevent future riots and lynchings. Wilson did not respond.

Furious with the president's silence, Walker told her hair-care agents at a meeting in August 1917 to talk to their communities about the "protest against wrong and injustice." She told them, "We should protest until the American sense of justice is so aroused that such affairs as the East St. Louis riot be forever impossible."

The group sent a telegram to Wilson, urging him to support laws that would help put a stop to riots and murders. The following month, Walker was elected vice president of the National Equal Rights League, founded in 1908 by William Monroe Trotter, an outspoken critic of racial inequality. Walker worked with her friend Ida Wells-Barnett on an anti-lynching campaign and on ways to end segregation and racial inequality.

In 1918, World War I ended. The Allied Powers, including the United States, defeated the Central Powers of Austria-Hungary, Germany, and others. In 1919, the Allies scheduled a conference in Paris to work out a peace settlement. The National Equal Rights League decided to hold its own peace conference in Paris at the same time—to protect the rights of black soldiers when they came back home. Walker and Wells-Barnett were selected as delegates to the convention.

Freeman Ransom, still the general manager of Walker's company, was alarmed. He believed the National Equal Rights League was too radical. He warned Walker in a letter not to participate in the convention in Paris. "You must always bear in mind that you have a large business, whereas the others who are going have nothing. … There are many ways in which your business can be circumscribed [lose power] and hampered … so as to practically put you out of business."

Ida Wells-Barnett was an American journalist and reformer.

Walker replied to Ransom in a letter dated February 4, 1919:

Dear Mr. Ransom:

Your arguments have been passionate indeed against my participation in the Paris peace conference meetings planned by Mr. Trotter. I agree it is best to try to change a system from within, but I thought Mrs. Ida Wells-Barnett and myself would have represented our race well in the talks overseas. My great fear is that the world will finally forge its peace treaties, but Negroes will be left out entirely.

Ransom was also concerned because Walker was part of the International League of Darker Peoples. He warned her about this group, too, and said there were people in it with whom she should not associate. His warning came too late, however. Military spies were already watching Walker because of her association with the group. Her application for a passport was denied, and most of the other group members who wanted to go to Paris also couldn't get passports. Eventually, Walker heeded Ransom's

warnings and resigned from the International League of Darker Peoples.

In Paris, world leaders created the Versailles Treaty to officially end World War I. But it didn't mention the rights of African-American soldiers. Over the next 40 years, racial prejudice would grow in the United States. The country would not take the issue of civil rights seriously until another generation of black leaders would usher in the civil rights movement in the 1960s. ℘

In 1919, Walker met with Japanese publisher S. Kuriowa (center), a member of the delegation to the Paris Peace Conference. They discussed having African-American representatives at this post-World War I meeting.

9 THE NEW YORK YEARS

❦

Two years before World War I ended, Madam Walker moved to New York City. It was rapidly becoming a popular place for African-Americans to live. Years before, in the late 1800s, many people had moved to the North to get away from racial prejudice in the South. During World War I, thousands more went north to find jobs in industries that were producing military ammunition and supplies. Many of them settled in New York City.

Because the city's African-American population was growing, Walker's daughter, Lelia, decided that this was a good place to set up a branch of Lelia College and a luxurious Walker hair parlor. Lelia was particularly interested in a section of New York City called Harlem. She persuaded her mother to buy a

Lelia Walker Robinson renovated an office and beauty salon in New York City to sell Walker products.

townhouse there in 1913. The area was a popular place for black artists, writers, musicians, doctors, lawyers, and other professionals to live and set up businesses.

Lelia spared no expense in remodeling the townhouse for the college and hair salon. Although Walker had always enjoyed spending money on Lelia and spoiling her with extravagant parties and expensive gifts, both Walker and Ransom were concerned about how much money Lelia was spending.

The Walker New York salon opened in January 1916 with a lavish reception.

To see for herself what her daughter was doing, Walker went to New York. She was amazed at what she saw and wrote to Ransom, "It is just impossible for me to describe it to you." She told how the hair

salon was elegantly decorated in soft grays, royal blues, and white marble. "The decorators said that of all the work they had done here in that line there is nothing equal to it, not even on Fifth Avenue." Instead of being upset, Walker was proud that Lelia's hair salon was better than the exclusive salons of successful businesswomen such as Elizabeth Arden and Helena Rubinstein, where wealthy white women flocked for expensive beauty treatments.

Lelia purchased two buildings next to the college and salon. She hired Vertner Woodson Tandy, one of New York state's first registered black architects, to combine all the buildings into one unit. Lelia lived there in elegance, along with her adopted daughter, Mae, and Madam Walker.

No one knows for sure how the Walkers met Mae. She lived in Indianapolis and often visited her grandmother, who lived across the alley from the Walkers' home. She probably ran errands for the Walker hair parlor. Madam Walker noticed her

> *A period of great African-American creativity flourished in the 1920s and 1930s, especially in the Harlem area of New York City. Blacks and whites alike came to hear great jazz musicians perform at Harlem's famous Apollo Theater and other clubs. Madam Walker's daughter, Lelia, who changed her name to A'Lelia in 1922, was at the center of this cultural activity. She converted one floor of her home into what she called the Dark Tower, a gathering place for artists, writers, musicians, intellectuals, and socialites.*

Mae Walker Robinson was Madam C.J. Walker's adopted granddaughter.

beautiful, thick braided hair, and Mae became a model for Madam Walker's hair products.

Mae was very intelligent. Although she was a good student, her family hadn't been able to afford to send her to high school. Most people at the time did not go beyond elementary school. Madam Walker and Lelia became very fond of Mae, and she of them.

Lelia, who was separated from her husband and had no children, wanted to adopt Mae. She asked the girl's family for permission to make Mae her daughter. Knowing this would give Mae opportunities she would not get otherwise, the family agreed. In 1912, at the age of 13, Fairy Mae Bryant became Mae Walker Robinson, Lelia's adopted daughter and Madam Walker's adopted granddaughter. Suddenly, Mae found herself lifted from a place of poverty into the Walker world of wealth and luxury.

In the Harlem townhouse, Mae was surrounded by the best furniture, artwork, rugs, and tapestries that money could buy. Music also filled the house. It was obvious that Madam Walker and Lelia loved music—they owned a gold Victrola phonograph and gold-trimmed musical instruments, including a large organ, a grand piano, and a harp.

Madam Walker became famous in New York City. She was well-known as a high-society hostess, a person who invites famous people to lavish dinners and parties at her home. People considered it an honor to receive an invitation to her Harlem townhouse.

Then Madam Walker did something that amazed blacks and whites alike. She bought 4 ½ acres (1.8 hectares) of land in a very expensive area along the Hudson River. Her plan was to build a fabulous mansion. Her neighbors would be white millionaires

Madam C.J. Walker and her daughter Lelia entertained many people in the lobby of their Harlem townhouse.

such as oil tycoon John D. Rockefeller.

But while Walker was at the peak of her wealth and fame, she began having health problems. She was exhausted by her constant travels, and her doctor urged her to take time to rest. But it wasn't until her car was almost hit by a freight train that she was frightened enough to slow down and relax.

She went to Hot Springs, Arkansas, where spas were built around the area's natural mineral springs. She checked into a hotel and bathhouse and promised her doctors she would give up her hectic schedule. Walker's problems were caused by more than exhaustion, however. She was suffering from high blood pressure and the early stages of kidney disease.

Walker stayed in Hot Springs from November 1916 to February 1917. Like other wealthy Americans who visited there, Walker soaked in hot mineral baths and enjoyed relaxing massages. Wrapped in thick towels, she rested afterward in darkened rooms. Her health began to improve.

Feeling much better, she went back to her old ways. She plunged into her business and helped organizations that were protesting inequality against blacks. She also supervised the construction of her new mansion on the Hudson River. The designer was Tandy, the architect who had designed the Harlem salon and townhouse.

The estate would be huge and feature gardens and a pool. It reminded world-famous opera star Enrico Caruso of a villa in Italy, his home country. He suggested she name her estate Lewaro, which represented the first two letters in her daughter's full name: *LE*lia *WA*lker *RO*binson. Walker liked the idea, and the mansion on the Hudson River became Villa Lewaro.

Walker's friend Enrico Caruso was one of the most famous tenors in the history of opera.

Walker regularly visited the huge house as it was being built. Sometimes she took friends along. When Ida Wells-Barnett was in New York for a National Equal Rights League convention, the two women drove out to see how construction was coming along. Wells-Barnett later wrote:

We drove out there almost every day, and I asked her on one occasion what on earth she would do with a thirty-room house. ... She said, "I want plenty of room in which to entertain my friends."

Rest was the one thing Walker seemed unable to do. In November 1917, her blood pressure was sky-high again. She was diagnosed with nephritis, an incurable kidney disease. Her doctor ordered her to check into a famous sanatorium in Battle Creek, Michigan, run by Dr. John Harvey Kellogg.

Walker took her doctor's advice. There she followed the rules—she exercised and ate a vegetarian diet, including Corn Flakes, a new health food cereal that Kellogg and his brother had created for their patients. However, when she left, she went back to eating what she considered a tastier high-fat diet. Her doctor urged her to retire and never work again, but Walker returned to her usual activities.

In 1918, Walker traveled throughout the Midwestern states on a three-month sales trip. She also visited military camps that housed black officers and enlisted men. She urged them to be brave and patriotic despite the discrimination they suffered. Walker firmly believed that the United States owed a debt of gratitude to African-American soldiers.

In June 1918, Villa Lewaro was finished, and Madam Walker moved in. It soon became a popular gathering place. When Harlem's 369th Army Regiment returned from World War I, Walker invited them to her mansion.

At the beginning of 1919, 51-year-old Walker was feeling quite tired. She resolved to rest more at her

villa. By the end of March, however, she was on the road again. After visiting her factory in Indianapolis, she headed to St. Louis to introduce a new line of skin-care products. She also looked forward to enjoying Easter Sunday at her old church, St. Paul's AME in St. Louis. By Good Friday, however, she was gravely ill.

A large group of Walker agents attended a National Convention of Walker Beauticians at Villa Lewaro.

The Monday after Easter, her kidneys were failing. She was taken back to Villa Lewaro in a private railroad car filled with flowers from well-wishers. She felt as though she didn't have long to live, but she thanked God for her many blessings and said, "My desire now is to do more than ever for my race. ... I can see what they need."

On May 25, 1919, the Associated Press spread the news that "the wealthiest negro woman in the United States, if not the entire world" had died. Lelia and Mae, who were in Central America, searched for the quickest way to get home for the funeral. They boarded the first available freight ship to New York, but the ship was delayed several hours. They arrived just hours after the funeral ended.

Thousands of mourners traveled by bus or car to Walker's funeral at Villa Lewaro. Many important African-Americans—from ministers and political activists to artists and teachers—paid their last respects to the woman who had risen from the cotton fields to the highest level of business success. Among the speakers was Mary McLeod Bethune. "She has gone," said Bethune of her friend, "but her work still lives and shall live as an inspiration to not only her race but to the world."

Madam C.J. Walker was buried in Woodlawn Cemetery in the Bronx district of New York City. Her memory is still honored by two historic landmarks: Villa Lewaro and the Madame Walker Theatre Center in Indianapolis. Her true legacy, however, is not in material

Like her mother, Lelia had high blood pressure. She died in 1931 at the age of 46. The Walker Manufacturing Company produced hair products until it was sold in 1986. As requested by her mother, Lelia willed Villa Lewaro to the NAACP. The house is now a National Historic Landmark.

In 1998, the
U.S. Postal
Service issued
a stamp in its
Black Heritage
series that
honored
Madam C.J.
Walker as
an outstand-
ing African-
American.

things but rather in the hope of a better life that she brought to thousands of African-American women. In addition, she left a vision of racial equality that helped change the world and inspire future generations. ✿

WALKER'S LIFE

1867
Born December 23 in Delta, Louisiana

1873
Mother, Minerva Breedlove, dies; father, Owen Breedlove, dies in 1875

1878
Moves to Vicksburg, Mississippi, and lives with her sister Louvenia

1875

1867
Russia sells Alaska to the United States

1876
Alexander Graham Bell makes the first successful telephone transmission

1879
Thomas Edison invents electric lights

WORLD EVENTS

1885

1885
Daughter Lelia
is born

1882
Marries Moses
McWilliams; moves
into her own home

1887
Husband Moses
McWilliams dies

1886
Grover Cleveland
dedicates the Statue
of Liberty in New
York Harbor, a gift
from the people
of France

1884
The first practical
fountain pen is
invented by Lewis
Edson Waterman, a
45-year-old American
insurance broker

WALKER'S LIFE

1889

Moves with daughter to St. Louis, Missouri

1894

Marries John Davis, from whom she would separate after nine years

1905

Moves to Denve Colorado; devel formula for her Wonderful Hair Grower

1900

1889

The Eiffel Tower opens in France

1903

Brothers Orville and Wilbur Wright successfully fly a powered airplane

WORLD EVENTS

1908

Moves to Pittsburgh, Pennsylvania; opens a hair parlor and Lelia College to train agents

)06

arries C.J. Walker; vels to promote r products and cruit sales agents

1910

Moves to Indianapolis, Indiana; buys a home and builds a factory

1910

)06

arthquake and fires stroy most of San rancisco; more than 000 people die

1909

The National Association for the Advancement of Colored People (NAACP) is founded

WALKER'S LIFE

1911

Incorporates the Walker Manufacturing Company; donates money to the YMCA

1912

Divorces her third husband; daughter adopts Mae Walker Robinson

1913

Buys a townhouse in New York City

1912

The *Titanic* sinks on its maiden voyage; more than 1,500 people die

1913

Henry Ford begins to use standard assembly lines to produce automobiles

WORLD EVENTS

1919

Dies May 25 at Villa Lewaro

1914–1915

Travels extensively, holding demonstrations and recruiting agents

1918

Moves to Villa Lewaro

1915

1914

Archduke Francis Ferdinand is assassinated, launching World War I (1914–1918)

1917

Vladimir Lenin and Leon Trotsky lead Bolsheviks in a rebellion against the Russian government during the October Revolution

NAME AT BIRTH: Sarah Breedlove

DATE OF BIRTH: December 23, 1867

BIRTHPLACE: Grand View plantation, Delta, Louisiana

FATHER: Owen Breedlove (1828?-1875)

MOTHER: Minerva Breedlove (1828?-1873)

EDUCATION: Self-educated and night classes

FIRST SPOUSE: Moses McWilliams (?-1887)

DATE OF MARRIAGE: 1882

CHILDREN: Lelia McWilliams Robinson (1885–1931)

SECOND SPOUSE: John Davis

DATE OF MARRIAGE: 1894

THIRD SPOUSE: Charles Joseph "C.J." Walker

DATE OF MARRIAGE: January 4, 1906

DATE OF DEATH: May 25, 1919

PLACE OF BURIAL: Woodlawn Cemetery, New York City

FURTHER READING

Bundles, A'Lelia Perry. *Madam C.J. Walker.* Philadelphia: Chelsea House Publishers, 1991.

Lommel, Cookie. *Madame C.J. Walker: Entrepreneur.* Los Angeles: Melrose Square Publishing Company, 1993.

McKissack, Lisa Beringer. *Women of the Harlem Renaissance.* Minneapolis: Compass Point Books, 2007.

Worth, Richard. *Beginning a New Life: African Americans During Reconstruction.* New York: Facts On File, 2006.

LOOK FOR MORE SIGNATURE LIVES BOOKS ABOUT THIS ERA:

Clara Barton: *Founder of the American Red Cross*

George Washington Carver: *Scientist, Inventor, and Teacher*

Amelia Earhart: *Legendary Aviator*

Thomas Alva Edison: *Great American Inventor*

Yo-Yo Ma: *Renowned Concert Cellist*

Thurgood Marshall: *Civil Rights Lawyer and Supreme Court Justice*

Annie Oakley: *American Sharpshooter*

Will Rogers: *Cowboy, Comedian, and Commentator*

Amy Tan: *Writer and Storyteller*

Booker T. Washington: *Innovative Educator*

On the Web

For more information on this topic, use FactHound.

1. Go to *www.facthound.com*
2. Type in this book ID: 0756518830
3. Click on the *Fetch It* button.

FactHound will find the best Web sites for you.

Historic Sites

Madame Walker Theatre Center
National Historic Landmark
617 Indiana Ave.
Indianapolis, IN 46202
317/236-2099
An establishment for the performing arts and museum on Walker's life and legacy; housed in the former Walker Manufacturing Company

Villa Lewaro National Historic Landmark
North Broadway
Irvington-on-Hudson, NY
(Not open to the public)
Mansion built by Madam C.J. Walker; a popular gathering place for prominent black leaders

abolitionist
a person who supported the banning of slavery

civil rights
a person's rights that are guaranteed by the U. S. Constitution

Confederacy
Southern states that fought against the Northern states in the Civil War

discrimination
unfair treatment of a person or group, usually because of race

foundries
buildings for molding melted metal into shapes

perseverance
the act of continually trying or committing to a certain action or belief

sanatorium
facility for rest or improving health

sharecropper
farmer who works the land in exchange for housing, food, and part of the profits

stock
the value of a company, divided into shares when sold to investors

trolley car
streetcar that runs on a track and is powered by electricity

vigilantes
people who punish lawbreakers personally and illegally rather than relying on legal authorities

Chapter 1

Page 9, line 1: A'Lelia Perry Bundles. *Madam C.J. Walker.* Chelsea House Publications, 1992, p. 71.

Page 9, line 5: Ibid.

Page 10, line 21: Ibid.

Chapter 3

Page 26, line 5: A'Lelia Perry Bundles. *On Her Own Ground: the Life and Times of Madam C.J. Walker.* Washington Square Press, 2002, p. 40.

Chapter 4

Page 29, line 2: Ibid., p. 43.

Page 33, line 18: Ibid., p. 32.

Page 35, line 1: Ibid., p. 68.

Chapter 5

Page 39, line 10: *Madam C.J. Walker,* p. 35.

Page 40, line 11: *On Her Own Ground: The Life and Times of Madam C.J. Walker,* p. 83.

Chapter 6

Page 46, line 9: Ibid., p. 98.

Page 47, line 2: Ibid.

Page 47, line 15: Ibid., p. 93.

Page 48, line 4: Ibid., p. 154.

Page 50, line 5: *Madam C.J. Walker,* p. 67.

Page 50, line 12: Ibid., p. 40.

Chapter 7

Page 53, line 12: Ibid., p. 101.

Page 54, line 5: Ibid., p. 100.

Page 54, line 13: Ibid., p. 101.

Page 56, line 21: Ibid., pp. 44-45.

Page 63, line 12: "A Brief History of the YMCA Movement." http://www.ymca.net/about_the_ymca/history_of_the_ymca.html

Page 65, line 8: *Madam C.J. Walker,* p. 71.

Page 67, line 19: *On Her Own Ground: The Life and Times of Madam C.J. Walker,* p. 77.

Page 68, line 24: Ibid., p. 122.

Page 70, line 1: Ibid., p. 134.

Page 71, line 2: Ibid., p. 135.

Page 72, line 1: Ibid.

Page 73, line 14: Ibid., p. 153.

Page 73, line 23: Ibid., p. 166.

Chapter 8

Page 80, line 15: Ibid., p. 212.

Page 81, line 20: *Madam C.J. Walker*, p. 98.

Page 82, line 3: Tananarive Due. *The Black Rose*. Random House, 2000, pp. 354-355.

Chapter 9

Page 86, line 14: *On Her Own Ground: The Life and Times of Madam C.J. Walker*, p. 146.

Page 91, line 23: Ibid., p. 215.

Page 93, line 13: Ibid., p. 269.

Page 94, line 2: Ibid., pp. 275-276

Page 94, line 16: *Madam C.J. Walker*, p. 100.

Select Bibliography

Bundles, A'Lelia Perry. *On Her Own Ground: The Life and Times of Madam C.J. Walker.* New York: Scribner, 2002.

Bundles, A'Lelia Perry. *Madam C.J. Walker.* New York: Chelsea House Publishers, 1991.

Due, Tananarive. *The Black Rose.* New York: Random House Publishing Group, 2000.

Lommel, Cookie. *Madame C.J. Walker: Entrepreneur.* Los Angeles: Melrose Square Publishing Company, 1993.

"Madame C.J. Walker (Sarah Breedlove)." *Contemporary Black Biography,* Gale Research. 1994. 28 July 2006. www.gale.com/free_resources/bhm/bio/walker_s.htm

"Walker, Sarah Breedlove." *Famous American Women.* Robert McHenry, ed. New York: Dover, 1980.

"Walker, Sarah Breedlove." *Notable American Women Vol. III.* Cambridge, Mass.: Belknap Press of Harvard University, 1971.

advertising, 40, 42
African Methodist Episcopal (AME) Church, 30–31, 39, 45
agents, 10, 13, 34, 45, 46, 48, 49, 50, 57, 61, 65, 80
Apex Hair and News Company, 10
Apollo Theater, 87
Arden, Elizabeth, 87

Battle Creek, Michigan, 92
Bethel African Methodist Episcopal Church, 55, 56
Bethune, Mary McLeod, 60–61, 94
Bethune-Cookman College, 60, 61
Black Exodus, 27
Black Freemasons, 32
Breedlove, Alex (brother), 20–21, 25–26, 29–30, 33
Breedlove, James (brother), 20–21, 25–26, 29–30
Breedlove, Louvenia (sister), 17, 23, 26, 27, 33
Breedlove, Minerva (mother), 15, 16, 18
Breedlove, Owen (father), 15, 16, 18
Breedlove, Owen, Jr. (brother), 20–21, 25–26, 29–30
Breedlove, Sarah. *See* Walker, Madam C. J.
Brilliantine product, 41
Brokenburr, Robert Lee, 58, 59
Burney, Robert W., 16, 19

Caruso, Enrico, 91
Carver, George Washington, 68
Chaplin, Charlie, 75
Chicago, Illinois, 69
cholera, 20
Civil Rights Act (1871), 77
civil rights movement, 83
Civil War, 15, 17–18, 18–19, 30
Cohron, Sarah, 32
Colored Knights of Pythias, 32
Corn Flakes, 92
cotton, 11, 15, 16, 20, 21, 27, 29

Cotton Club, 87
Court of Calanthe auxiliary, 32

Dark Tower, 87
Davis, John (husband), 33
Daytona Normal and Industrial Institute for Negro Girls 60
Delta, Louisiana, 15, 17–18
Denver, Colorado, 35, 37–38, 40
discrimination, 76, 77, 92
Division of Negro Affairs (National Youth Administration), 61
DuBois, W. E. B., 67, 76–77, 78

East St. Louis, Illinois, 78, 80
education, 15, 19, 20, 27, 31, 60, 61, 64, 65, 68, 88
Ellington, Duke, 87
employees. *See* agents.

factory. *See* Walker Manufacturing Company.
Fisk University, 82
Food and Drug Act (1906), 47

Glossine product, 41
Grand View plantation, 15, 16, 18, 19
Grant, Ulysses S., 19, 77

Hampton Institute, 67
Hampton, Virginia, 67
Harlem, New York, 85–87, 88–89
Hot Springs, Arkansas, 90

Indianapolis Freeman newspaper, 56
Indianapolis, Indiana, 55, 56–57, 63, 73, 75, 87, 93, 94
International League of Darker Peoples, 82, 83
investors, 53, 54
Isis Theater, 75–76

Kansas, 24–25, 27
Kellogg, John Harvey, 92
Kelly, Alice, 61–62

Knox, George L., 56, 69–70
Knoxville College, 37, 43
Ku Klux Klan, 77, 78

Lelia College, 49, 85
lynchings, 77, 78, 80, 82

Madam C. J. Walker Hair Culturists
    Union of America, 10
Madam C. J. Walker Manufacturing
    Company, 51, 53, 54–55, 57, 58,
    62, 94
Madam C. J. Walker's Wonderful Hair
    Grower, 39, 41–42
Madam Walker Hair Culture Method,
    9–10, 12–13, 42, 49
Madam Walker Theatre Center, 94
McWilliams, Moses (husband), 26, 27
McWilliams, Sarah. *See* Walker,
    Madam C. J.
Mississippi River, 18, 19, 20, 25
Moody Bible Institute, 61

National Association for the
    Advancement of Colored People
    (NAACP), 78, 94
National Association of Colored
    Women, 60
National Convention of Madam C. J.
    Walker Agents, 65
National Equal Rights League, 80, 81
National Negro Business League, 64,
    65, 69–72
National Youth Administration, 61
Negro Farmers' Conference, 68
nephritis, 92
New York City, New York, 85, 94

Oberlin College, 32

patent medicines, 47
Philadelphia, Pennsylvania, 10, 65
Pittsburgh, Pennsylvania, 48–49, 51
Pope-Turnbo, Annie, 10, 34
Poro Company, 10, 34, 38

Powell, Jesse (brother-in-law), 23, 26, 27
Powell, Willie (nephew), 33

race riots, 78, 80
railroads, 48–49, 56
Ransom, Freeman B., 58, 59, 76,
    81–82, 82–83, 86
Reconstruction, 24
Reynolds, Violet Davis, 62–63, 75–76
Robinson, John, 51
Robinson, Lelia (daughter), 27, 29, 32,
    37, 43, 49, 50–51, 58, 75, 85–86,
    87, 88, 89, 94
Robinson, Mae Walker (granddaughter),
    87–88, 94
Rockefeller, John D., 90
Rubinstein, Helena, 87
Rust College, 82

Scholtz, Edmund L., 38–39
segregation, 77, 80
sharecroppers, 15–16
Singleton, Benjamin "Pap," 27
slavery, 15, 16, 30, 37–38, 49
social clubs, 31, 32, 40, 45, 49
St. Louis Colored Orphans Home, 32
St. Louis, Missouri, 25, 26, 29, 30, 38,
    40, 93
St. Paul African Methodist Episcopal
    (AME) Church, 30–31, 93
St. Paul's missionary society, 33
sulfur, 39

Tandy, Vertner Woodson, 87, 90
Trotter, William Monroe, 80, 82
tuberculosis, 20
Tuskegee Airmen, 68
Tuskegee Normal and Industrial
    Institute, 54, 64, 67, 68, 72
Tuskegee University, 68

Underground Railroad, 49, 56
Union Baptist Church, 10

Versailles Treaty, 83

Vicksburg, Mississippi, 18, 19, 21, 23, 24, 26, 27, 29
Villa Lewaro, 89–90, 90–91, 92, 94
voting rights, 19, 25, 82

Walker, Charles Joseph (husband), 40, 42, 45, 48, 55, 58, 64
Walker Hair Culture Method, 46
Walker, Madam C.J.
   African Methodist Episcopal (AME) Church and, 30–31, 39, 45
   African-American soldiers and, 78, 80, 81, 92
   anti-lynching campaign of, 80
   automobiles and, 75
   baldness of, 11, 34
   birth of, 15
   Booker T. Washington and, 54, 64, 65, 67–73, 76
   childhood of, 10, 11, 16–17, 20, 23–24
   death of, 94
   demonstrations by, 41–42, 42–43, 46–47, 59, 92
   education of, 20, 32, 61
   generosity of, 13, 33, 60–61, 63–64, 72, 77
   hair growth formula of, 12, 39, 62
   Harlem salon and, 86–87
   health of, 90, 92–93
   International League of Darker Peoples and, 82, 83
   marriages of, 26, 33, 40
   movies and, 75–76
   at National Negro Business League conference, 69–72
   networking of, 39–40, 45, 49, 55
   as Poro agent, 34–35, 38
   religious beliefs of, 30
   as sharecropper, 11, 16, 20
   silent march and, 78
   St. Paul's missionary society and, 33
   as vice president of National Equal Rights League, 80, 81–82
   Villa Lewaro and, 89–90, 90–91, 92, 94
   Walker Manufacturing Company and, 51, 53, 54–55, 57, 58, 62, 94
   as washerwoman, 11, 16–17, 20, 23–24, 30, 32, 33, 35, 39, 47–48, 71
   as widow, 27, 29
   Woodrow Wilson and, 78–80
Walker Manufacturing Company, 51, 53, 54–55, 57, 58, 62, 94
Walker Method. See Madam Walker Hair Culture Method.
Walker's Sore Wash, 45
Walker's Sure Cure Blood and Rheumatic Cure, 45
Ward, Joseph, 55
Washington, Booker T., 54, 64, 65, 67–73, 76
Washington, Sarah Spencer, 10
Wells-Barnett, Ida, 80, 81, 82, 91
Wilson, Woodrow, 78–80
women's clubs, 32, 39–40
Woodlawn Cemetery, 94
World War I, 78, 81, 83, 85
World War II, 68

yellow fever, 20
Young Men's Christian Association (YMCA), 63–64, 72

Darlene R. Stille is the author of more than 80 books for young people, including collections of biographies. She grew up in Chicago and attended the University of Illinois, where she discovered her love of writing. She now lives and writes in Michigan.

Image Credits